SHABBY

THE JOLLY GOOD BRITISH GUIDE TO STRESS-FREE LIVING

JOSIE LLOYD
& EMLYN REES

CONSTABLE

CONSTABLE

First published in Great Britain in 2017 by Constable

Copyright © Josie Lloyd and Emlyn Rees, 2017

The moral right of the authors has been asserted.

A CIP catalogue record for this book
is available from the British Library.

ISBN: 978-1-47212-729-7

Cover and page design by Design23

Printed and bound in Italy by L.E.G.O. SpA

Papers used by Constable are from well-managed forests and other responsible sources.

Constable
An imprint of
Little, Brown Book Group
Carmelite House
50 Victoria Embankment
London EC4Y 0DZ

An Hachette UK Company
www.hachette.co.uk
www.littlebrown.co.uk

Photo credits: Shutterstock: pages 6, 12, 17 (top), 25 (bottom right), 27, 30 (top right), 34, 40, 53, 54 (top and bottom), 56/57 (middle). ALAMY: pages 5, 8, 11, 13 (top right and bottom left), 15, 18, 19, 20/21, 22, 23, 24, 25, 26, 30 (bottom left), 31, 32, 33, 35, 38, 39, 41, 42, 43, 44, 45, 46, 48, 49, 51, 52, 54 middle, 55, 56/57 (top and bottom), 59, 60, 61, 62, 63. iStock: Page 12 (top left) monkybusinessimages/iStock, 14 ROMAOSLO/iStock, 17 (bottom left) Bosca78/iStock, 28 MagMos/iStock, 29 dstaerk/iStock, 30 (top left) misscherrygolightly/iStock, 30 (bottom right) zeleno/iStock, 36 frmate/iStock, 50 Magmos/iStock

CONTENTS

WHAT IS SHABBY?

Shabby (pronounced sh-abē) is the quintessential British lifestyle and aesthetic movement deriving from the ancient British philosophy of 'Shabbism'.

Shabbism |ˈsh-ab-izəm|
Noun
The belief system revolving around the core principle that life's just too bloody short to waste time striving for perfection and worrying too much about what other people think.

Examples:
1) **Sarah and Sam are total Shabbists. They only dust the front of ornaments and never higher than their tallest friend's line of sight.**

2) **Dave and Mandy are Shabby, but not scuzzy. They always make sure they flip their baby-milk-stained sofa cushions over to the cleaner 'Guest' side whenever their parents come round.**

Derivatives:
Shabbist |ˈsh-ab-ist| noun, a practitioner of Shabbism
Shabby |ˈsh-abē| adjective, the way of the Shabbist
Shabbiness |ˈsh-abē-nes| noun, the goal of the Shabbist
Shabbification |ˈsh-ab-i-fik-ā-sh-ən| noun, metamorphosis towards Shabbiness

Origin mid-fourteenth century: from dialect shab [scab] (meaning 'itch')

THE FOUR PILLARS OF SHABBISM

1. MESSINESS

2. DILAPIDATION

3. CLUTTER

4. BODGED WORKS

On a macro level, Shabbists believe that a 'lived-in' look and attitude promotes harmony and inner contentment via its innate rejection of social competitiveness and materialism, thereby enhancing human interconnectivity and spiritual wellbeing on a universal scale.

On a micro level, Shabbists also believe this means you spend a lot less time fussing and tidying up and getting stressed about stuff and nonsense that doesn't really matter anyway. Leaving you much more time to hang out with your family and friends.

WHAT SHABBY IS MOST CERTAINLY NOT

HYGGE

This unpronounceable Danish lifestyle trend of nurturing a cosy atmosphere by adorning one's home with fresh flower petals, neatly-folded blankets and lit candles could not be less Shabby if it tried. Shabby does not nurture. It simply is. The crisp packets, single socks and broken toys left by Shabby children on the living room floor have not been artfully scattered. They've just been dropped. Whilst leaving lit candles and neatly-folded anything around a Shabby home would prove highly problematic and traumatic. Problematic, because the chance of finding a lighter that actually works amongst all the other tat in the kitchen drawer is less than zero. And traumatic because exposing one's blankets to public scrutiny would involve admitting to moths.

LAGOM

Another Nordic lifestyle trend, translating literally as 'enough, sufficient, just right', but also deriving from the Swedish proverb 'Lagom är bäst', meaning 'enough is as good as a feast'. Such Lutheran self-denial clearly has no place in a Shabby home. Shabbists believe quite the reverse. There can never be enough: defunct printers in the attic, tins of dried and drying paint in the shed, mismatched Tupperware lids and boxes in the kitchen drawer, tubes of almost finished toothpaste beside the sink. Less is not more, where Shabbists are concerned. More is more. More stuff lying around that might still come in handy one day. More time to yourself that you haven't wasted tidying up and fixing stuff that was already perfectly happy as it was.

MINIMALISM

From the life-changing magic of decluttering your home, to Japanese knicker-rolling tips, to the cavernously nihilistic, granite and steel homes of the European über-rich, all forms of minimalism are anathema to the Shabbist. Far from minimalism, a Shabbist's goal is maximalism. He or she seeks a life that is not empty, but splendidly cluttered and full.

> Far from minimalism, a Shabbist's goal is maximalism. He or she seeks a life that is not empty, but splendidly cluttered and full.

CLEANISM

Of course everyone and everything needs a good wash and scrub every now and then, and there's a clear line between shabbiness and grubbiness (the same line that appears on the side of the bath once the water's been let out). But all too often the quest for basic hygiene can spill over into fastidiousness and a general dislike of the human condition in all its naturally grubby, creased and wrinkly glory. Shabbists believe we must resist this sparkling, Evian-esque tide of cleanism lapping at the shores of our homes, clothes and very beings. Meaning it's a big *no* to dry-cleaning your work shirts, a nauseated *sod off* to kale shakes, and an outraged *you are bloody joking, right?* to vaginal steaming. While drip-drying your clothes, gobbling down last night's reheated takeaway curry, and having a jolly good soak every once in a while, all receive a heartening and resoundingly Shabby *yes*.

SHINISM

Adherents of Shinism, known as 'Shinies', are the natural foe of Shabbists everywhere. Shinies personify everything a Shabbist is emphatically not. Everything about them is tidy and smart and looks suspiciously and ostentatiously new. Imagine a factory-fresh, shop-window dummy, sporting this season's latest fashions, whilst taking a selfie featuring its own orthodontically perfect grin, in a featureless, clutter-free, symmetrical, pristine, polished concrete room, within a brutalist, modernist building that's been recently vacuumed and filled with ionically purified air. And that's your average Shiny right there. Shinies are not part of life, but apart from it, or so Shabbists fervently believe. And their diabolical aberrations and blasphemies run deep. Some are even rumoured to have separate pairs of scissors for doing school projects and cutting their nails.

SHABBY AT HOME

The home is where the Shabby aesthetic really comes to life. Don't be fooled that the much-sought-after Shabby air of gentle yet charming decay is easy to come by. That 'slightly grubby, lived-in' feeling so cherished by Shabbists takes time and effort.

Most purists choose to shabbify their homes in a traditional manner, by wearing them in themselves over many years. But Interior Un-designers – also known as 'teenagers' – are increasingly popular on the scene, and can 'de-shiny' any home, or indeed any borrowed item of clothing or vehicle, in a surprisingly short amount of time.

> A house is a home, not a temple, which is why all Shabbists choose to wear their shoes on the inside.

THE SHABBY WELCOME

You will know straight away that you are in a Shabby home from the communal areas, all of which should have dim lighting, due to one or several missing light bulbs.

On arrival, the mat will be littered with pizza flyers and often there will be a welcoming pair of pants on the radiator. The bottom stair should always house a pile of unopened mail, mainly from banks and credit-card companies. The proper finishing touch is for the actual hallway to be virtually impassable, due to a multiple pile-up of buggies, bikes, skateboards, and even an occasional disconsolate and immovable child. A bulging bin-bag, which has yet to be put out, makes for a pleasing additional welcoming touch on the front porch.

Shabbists are not entirely insensitive to the standards and expectations of others – particularly those who might not be of a Shabby persuasion themselves. Often Shabbists will greet newcomers with a sheen of perspiration from the manic household tidy-up which has taken place in the half an hour preceding their guests' arrival. Such clean-a-thons are, of course,

The radiator is mentioned here, but communal areas will rarely be hot, or even vaguely warm, in a Shabby home, which is, by its very decrepit nature, fairly open to the elements. Hardcore traditionalists will only put the heating on when it's needed to crack the ice in the loo. Even amateurs will usually wait until there's at least a 'Decem' in the month.

A GENERAL NOTE CONCERNING THE SHABBIST CONCEPT OF UN-
Not to be confused with the Buddhist om, un- is a sacred sound and spiritual icon integral to the understanding of Shabbism. It is only through the use of un- that we are able to explore many of the unique concepts central to Shabby living, which the English language otherwise fails to describe. These include the many items and places that a Shabbist will encounter during their life which are un-useful, un-stressful, un-matching, un-emptied, un-roadworthy, un-enterable, un-bagged and un-found.

short-lived in their effectiveness, with the Shabbist's home often reverting to its normal, easy-going, messy state within minutes of a guest's arrival. But – hey-ho – it's the thought that counts. Plus the very presence of the guest during the transformation from tidy to un- means they're at least partly to blame themselves, so certainly not in any position to complain.

And whilst Shabbists are extremely tolerant of the degree of messiness in their own abodes, even they will admit that some excesses can get out of control and tip over into scuzziness. Being completely unable to see the floor of a child's bedroom due to 'shed' clothing, for example, is going too far, and a weekly 'sort-it-out' is to be encouraged. Similarly, being able to 'dust graffiti' messages on your TV screen with your fingertip is clearly beyond the pale, as it can compromise the enjoyment of such classic Shabby shows as *Poldark* and the *Antiques Roadshow*.

The Hall Carpet

A 'multi-texture', stained hall carpet provides a perfect Shabby welcome. Unless you're lucky enough to inherit one, this effect can only really be achieved through years of carelessly treading dirt into the home, as well as taking such standardised precautionary measures as ensuring that hot and cold beverages – especially of the milky, chocolate-y and blackcurrant-y kind – are carried around the house by small children without adult supervision. Amateur Shabbists seeking this effect must always be careful never to 'over-stain', in case their guests mistake their careful soiling for an actual factory 'pattern'.

The shoe-thingy is the home for other essential household items, such as sunglasses with only one arm.

The 'Shoe-Thingy'

Prominently displayed in the most public area of the home, a true Shabbist will proudly present the household's entire collection of shoes – old and new. In the immediate vicinity of this tangled collection will be an item of furniture – often referred to as a 'shoe-tree' or 'shoe-thingy' – but all shoes must always remain outside this vestibule. Instead, the shoe-thingy is the home for other essential household items, such as sunglasses with only one arm, single gloves, torn umbrellas and novelty hats, and is also frequently the hiding place for the plastic key needed to open the electricity meter box (see also 'The Kitchen Drawer').

The Coat Rack

Also in the welcoming area of the home, the coat rack must always be maintained at maximum capacity for the proper effect, so that coats can only be hung by someone possessing an in-depth knowledge of physics and/or Buckaroo. (Individuals lacking these skills, including all children, should content themselves with simply flinging their garments in the general direction of the rack and watching them fall to the floor.) To achieve this effect, the rack's pegs must be bulked out with obsolete sweatshirts and seldom-worn fashion mackintoshes. It can also be achieved by putting bicycle helmets on the pegs, to ensure that nothing else can be usefully hung.

A GENERAL NOTE FOR FIRST-TIME VISITORS TO A SHABBY HOME

To fully appreciate 'Shabbification', the natural process through which a home becomes truly Shabby over time, always remember to look up. It's something Shabbists themselves rarely do. In fact, many outsiders question whether Shabbists, like dogs, are actually capable of looking up at all. Which is a great shame, because in the heights of any Shabby dwelling, the beauty of Shabbism is right there to behold. Qualities to look for include dust-clogged lampshades, 'candelabras' and 'stalactites' of cobwebs, and – if you're tall enough – thick 'fingers' of age-old 'leak crystallisation', pointing along cornices to mortar cracks. Depending on the home in question, and the season, you may also be lucky enough to spot evidence of 'de-snagging', that mystical process so revered by Shabbists, whereby the truly Shabby home begins to shed all remnants of its own originally shiny decoration. Peer hard enough into the corners and you could catch glimpses of speckled, peeling paper, mouldy plaster, and all the other glorious telltale signs of incurable creeping damp. Or if you're really in luck, you might even witness the beginning of a sagging ceiling, heralding an imminent structural collapse.

THE SHABBY LIVING ROOM

This is a happy room where the Shabbist likes to kick back, relax and snuggle up with assorted children and pets on the sofa. This is where games are played, family discussions take place and an in-depth critique of what's on the telly is enacted. The living room in a Shabby home may not, on first inspection, immediately reveal its identifying Shabby traits, but look a little closer and you'll hopefully soon find some classics.

Windows & Curtains

Other than the perpetually flaking, rattling window frames to which they're invariably attached, Shabby curtains or blinds might initially look perfectly normal, but up close they'll soon be discovered to be ripped and frayed along the bottom from old age and animal intervention (see also 'Shabby Pets'). Curtain tops will show signs of intermittent sagging, also known as 'concertina-ing', due to missing hooks. Meanwhile, the window panes themselves should be grimy enough to convince anyone peering out that it's a real 'pea-souper', even on a hot, sunny day.

The Living Room Rug

The living room rug may also appear superficially clean, but will in fact hide the remnants of several takeaways, missing batteries, and several pieces from the Monopoly set. It is also the home to the only needle in the Shabby house and, as such, inspires regular bouts of agonised screaming and recriminations from whoever the 'lucky' person is who's just found it.

The Sofa

To achieve the correct look, the sofa cushions must never retain their original shape or position, and both armrests must sport an 'Olympic Ring Effect' of mug- and glass-bottom stains. Sofa cushions should in addition have designated 'Family' and 'Guest' sides, the latter being marginally less stained with baby milk, Marmite and chicken korma than the former, and which should only be displayed when in the company of extremely important guests, such as one's mother-in-law or the Pope. Beneath the cushions, there should be a sizeable area dedicated to loose change, Kirby grips, advertisements from Sunday papers, un-won lottery scratch cards, sweet wrappers, odd socks and missing batteries. The sofa is also often the focal point of a perennial Shabbist discussion, the gist of which is to declare that it's really time to get a new sofa, but then to think of reasons why not, including what on earth are you going to do with the old one, and what's the point anyway because the kids and pets will only ruin the new one as soon as it arrives. Yet another example of the much-favoured Shabby trait of procrastination.

The Remote Control

Pure Shabbists will always have a remote control with one battery missing (for official Shabby hiding places for batteries, please also see 'The Sofa' and 'The Living Room Rug').

Novice Shabbists often make the error of using tape to attempt to keep the batteries in place after the initial loss or breaking of the device's original plastic cover. They soon discover, however, that the high level of dust particles at large in the Shabby environment means that tape loses its stickiness within minutes, if not seconds, of application.

Sofa cushions should have designated 'Family' and 'Guest' sides, the latter being marginally less stained with baby milk and chicken korma.

Tech both new and old should be a centrepiece of any Shabbist living room. Wires should be both tangled and stretched across the full extent of the room wherever possible, to give it that highly sought-after 'student' or 'laboratory' feel. Obsolete technology such as combo DVD and VHS players and cracked and burned-out games consoles should be kept near or behind or on top of the TV – forever waiting for that oft-promised but never-realised trip to the Great Loft in the Sky.

It's the little touches that make all the difference. Remnants of Christmas decorations can help to provide a pleasingly festive atmosphere the whole year round.

The Toy Box

The toy box provides another perfect illustration of the process of 'Shabbification' (see also 'Note For First-Time Visitors'), whereby any given home becomes increasingly Shabby over time. This receptacle is customarily of modest size and is purchased upon the arrival of a Shabbist's first child, in the naïve and mistaken belief that this is where all the toys and other childhood paraphernalia will be kept. Though in reality, of course, it's only a matter of days before these same items begin their inevitable 'multiplication' and 'migration' across the entire Shabby home.

Shabby Treasures

The kitchen is the beating heart of the Shabby home, and as such should be a veritable Guggenheim of 'Shabby Treasures', being items of no monetary or practical use whatsoever, which nonetheless remain much cherished and impossible to throw out, because they might have once belonged to a favourite aunt, or were made by one of the kids, or could even possibly get fixed one day, if one could only find the time.

Such items range from the grand to the mundane, and might include once valuable (but now cracked) china platters, crystal glass decanters (dulled to a sticky opaque blood-red with the remnants of last year's port that never quite got washed out), teetering stacks of records and CDs (most missing, scratched or in the wrong sleeves), giant collections of cheese sauce- and

> 'You can't make an omelette without breaking a few eggs. Particularly if you can't even find the eggs.'

19

gravy-splattered cookery books, as well as the children's school certificates and supermarket vouchers. Especially when the children in question have long since had children of their own, and the supermarkets, with their tempting offers of half-price Opal Fruits and Jif, have ceased trading decades ago.

Shabbists like to have everything on show whenever possible, making things easier to find – from all of last month's Sunday papers, to all the 'best' china and glassware that never actually gets used.

The Fruit Bowl
Fruit doesn't live in the fridge; it should be left to ripen gloriously in the bowl. At all times, there should be at least one (half-mouldy, but perfectly gin-and-tonic worthy) lemon on display, as well as bananas that have gone an appetising shade of brown.

The Kitchen Units
There's also plenty of scope for bodged works in the Shabbist kitchen. In particular, pay close attention to cupboard and drawer fronts, several of which should be broken (often from piqued 'drawer jerking' sessions, which occur when drawers have become so full they can no longer be opened at all). Unit panels will usually also sport signs of bodged paint jobs, where the wrong colour paint has been mistakenly applied (also known as 'Picassos').

Very often, hidden somewhere inside a Shabby kitchen will be a Shabby booby-trap (see also 'The Shabby Garden'). An overstuffed cupboard that a newcomer might innocently 'trigger' at their peril. Or a window blind that always, without warning, collapses with ear-shattering effect.

The Kitchen Sink & Surfaces
Hygiene (see also 'Note On Shabby Hygiene' and 'Cleanism') in a Shabby kitchen is, admittedly, on the 'lower side of normal', but Shabbists often have stonkingly robust immune systems as a result. Anti-bacterial spray is not welcomed, and cleaning products – other than solid soap, carbolic soap and bleach – should be used sparingly and with suspicion. Especially any

that might mask the kitchen's otherwise more glorious odours of Stilton soup and dog.

Pots & Pans

Pots and pans are rarely fully clean, due to the decrepitude of the 1990s dishwasher (a prerequisite of any Shabby home), which specialises in 'kilning' remnants of porridge and scrambled eggs onto saucepans. As a result, there should be a teetering pile of washing-up in the sink at all times, ever threatening to cacophonously collapse.

The Kettle

The Shabby kettle should always have that friendly 'good morning' rattle, due to the build-up of limescale flakes inside, which has the additional benefit of making the tea taste pleasantly of tin.

Kitchen Storage

The Shabby home's cupboards are generally full of a haphazard selection of chipped mugs and crockery arranged in 'towers of Pisa'. Jammed alongside these and taking up all additional space are a multitude of rarely or never used un-useful items, including unwanted gifts and heirlooms, such as olive dishes, novelty soup bowls, fish kettles and cast-iron fondue sets. None of which, of course, can be thrown out, due to sentimental value (see also 'Shabby Treasures') and the innate optimism of the Shabbist that one day they will indeed be used.

Kitchen Appliances

They are old. Always. But often surprisingly fully functioning. It's not unusual to find a Shabbist who will proudly proclaim that their washing machine or dishwasher is twenty-five years old (see also 'Pots & Pans' above). In a Shabby kitchen, cookers and fridges often last for decades too. This is because they are never interfered with by professional cleaners and are never turned off at the wall – particularly the fridge and freezer, which are left to their own devices, even during long holidays, and are rarely fully explored, particularly in the freezer's more icy regions, where long-forgotten tubs of yellowing vanilla ice cream and homemade lollies are stored.

It is also the Shabby way never to throw away kitchen appliances that have seemingly reached the end of their working lives. These bulky and defunct but once much-lauded machines stay in the home for as long as possible, sometimes migrating to the garage or shed, along with the evergreen intention of one day getting them fixed.

The kitchen table should be both messy and cluttered, as well as dilapidated and bodged.

The Kitchen Table

This must display all tenets of Shabbism at all times. It should be both messy and cluttered, dilapidated and bodged, both above and below, a veritable compost heap of newspapers, school books, recent shopping, dog biscuits and rogue cutlery, as well as important 'to do' lists, which must not be lost, but which – by the very fact of their being in this pile – always are lost.

If cloth-free, the table will have a huge amount of toast and crumpet crumbs wedged into its joins. Most often wooden and stained, it will be perpetually in sore need of a varnish, which will never, ever occur. Modern Shabbists often deploy highly patterned oilcloths to cover their tables, patterns that only become more riotous with time, as felt-tip pen doodles, strawberry-jam smears, and three-dimensional 'Braille-trails' of dried tomato ketchup are added to its heady brew.

Creaking and at perpetual risk of imminent collapse, the table's legs should be warped, scratched and, preferably, gnawed (see also 'Shabby Pets').

Amateur Shabbists often start with The Kitchen Drawer, as the Shabby effect is so easy to achieve.

The Kitchen Drawer

Please note that this section refers to The Kitchen Drawer, not just any kitchen drawer. The Kitchen Drawer is the one where Shabbists genuinely believe 'all missing things reside'. Whilst this is regularly demonstrated to be completely untrue, it's a belief that remains fervent nonetheless. Amateur Shabbists often start with The Kitchen Drawer, as the Shabby effect is so easy to achieve. The Kitchen Drawer must be obstructed from closing at all times due to its nigh-on overwhelming volume of miscellaneous items.

At base level, The Kitchen Drawer must include: sets of old keys (preferably from previous homes), radiator keys, the plastic key needed to open the electricity meter box (see also 'The Shoe-Thingy'), balding hairbrushes, ancient takeaway menus from long-defunct eateries, loose foreign change in currencies that are no longer valid, such as the drachma and sesterce, a plethora of stationery, including unsharpened pencils and leaking biros, as well as defunct phone chargers and dead batteries (see also 'The Remote Control').

In a thrilling example of 'Shabbification' (see also 'Note For First-Time Visitors'), the Shabby effect of The Kitchen Drawer can slowly 'migrate' into all the other kitchen drawers over time. For example, the utensil drawer, or cutlery drawer, once specialist areas, can soon become home to such anomalies as stray toothbrushes, hairbands and old fuses.

The Fridge
As all true Shabbists know, many pickles and sauces can last forever and should be stored in the fridge with their lids only half on and preferably glued to the shelf with their own congealed, dripping residue. One of the pure joys of Shabby living is rediscovering an old favourite pickle from way back when. Preferably with a splinter of poppadum or cheese cracker still in it from its last outing.

The Cooker
The correct Shabby etiquette is for the cooker to be completely left alone to form its own greasy biosphere. Drawers at the bottom of the cooker should be wedged shut with rusty cake tins. Lighting the cooker should require a specialist technique, known only to a few, and never shared with guests. Its hood lights should never work – leading to a wonderful sense of mystery and occasional discovery whenever cooking – and its fan's motor should either rattle like a lawnmower, or be so clogged up that it's incapable of disturbing even a feather.

The Food Cupboard
In the Shabbist's food cupboard, the aim is never to throw any packet away – in particular packets of flour or pasta with an unusably small amount of product left inside (see also 'Shabby Eating'). Tinned goods are catnip to a true Shabbist, who on request will proudly be able to produce a tin of pilchards or plum tomatoes from the last century. There should also be many, many, almost-empty bottles of vinegar, as well as cereal boxes with just the scrumpled-up packet left inside. Home-produced marmalade, jam and jars of other delights (some dating back for decades, and often containing damsons and prunes) should help bulk out the food cupboard so that there is never actually any shelf space for

Lighting the cooker should require a specialist technique, known only to a few, and never shared with guests.

the shopping, which should always be added to the pile on the kitchen table instead
(see also 'The Kitchen Table').

The Spice Rack

The Shabbist is always proud to give plenty of kitchen display space to spice jars,
containing unidentifiable and tasteless powders and a semi-shaved ball of decades-
old nutmeg. The actual spices used for cooking are in open packets, going stale,
precariously stacked in the food cupboard. Preferably behind the empty cereal
packets, where they cannot be seen.

The Tupperware Cupboard

All Shabbists know that a whole cupboard in any kitchen must be dedicated to
Tupperware. The trick is to have many more lids than bottoms and for absolutely
none of them to fit each other.

The Warm Patch

The Shabby Kitchen will have one warm patch. This will be a radiator or an Aga rail, or somewhere the sun warms up. This coveted place is where the cat and/or dog sleeps, or small children snuggle up. Guests who attempt to hog it should be wary – there will always be stains.

The Utility Room

No doubt once envisaged as part of a utopian, futuristic domestic dream, the utility room of the Shabbist has long since shrunk in ambition to a place of dark mystery, a murky funk of pet smells and washing detergent, where ancient boilers clank, tumble dryers thud and sticky irons hiss, and where unwanted and new-fangled gifts, such as rowing machines and bread- and yoghurt-makers, lie wedged and forever un-found in corners between the dog basket and the guinea-pig cage.

A GENERAL NOTE ON SHABBY AMBIENCE (aka 'Shambience')

Shabbists like background noise. Along with the squeaks, purring and door scraping of their many pets and children, they often have the radio on all the time (and most usually tuned to Radio 4). However, as lots of music is on display in the kitchen (CDs and records), there is also ample opportunity for spontaneous dancing, often to tunes so scratched that the younger members of the family believe these warped sounds to be part of the original recordings themselves.

THE SHABBY BEDROOM

All skilled Shabbists enjoy the challenge and thrill of transforming a humble bedroom into a scene resembling a plane crash. Particularly gratifying is a hotel bedroom that can be trashed with an exploding suitcase in a matter of seconds too.

But the Shabby bedroom at home often needs nurturing over a longer period to achieve the desired effect. Particular attention to dust is always required, especially under the bed. The untouched deeper recesses of wardrobes and drawers should also be a breeding ground for jumper-chomping moths (see also 'Shabby Fashion' and 'Shabby Pets').

The Bed
A Shabbist's bed should remain un-made or 'sort-of'-made at all times (until guests come round, or there's a house or flat viewing, when it's actually tucked in, plumped and straightened). To achieve the right effect, the mattress must be at least a decade old and rest on struts, several of which are either missing or bunched up together, ensuring a bad night's sleep and regular bouts of 'Shabbist back'. Pillows must be

yellow with age and lumpy, and the fitted sheets must always be one size too small and remain un-tucked at one corner at least. At no time should the bed ever sport a set of matching bedsheets (see also 'The Shabby Landing'). Beneath the bed (also known in Shabbist circles as 'The Netherland'), the Shabbist may store rolls of unused Christmas wrapping paper and single slippers. It should not, however, be entirely cluttered. But rather, it should retain a proportion of designated space for 'extra cluttering', which will be needed at such times when all the other stuff scattered across the bedroom floor has to be tidied up or concealed at short notice.

Shabbists love a regular lie-in, but invariably the bed turns into a communal area for children and pets to snuggle up in too. The bed is also the place where all family members congregate to open hastily-wrapped birthday presents and Christmas stockings.

The Bedside Table

The purpose of the bedside table is to house as many of the mugs and glasses in the house as possible, preferably with a centimetre of tea or coffee and a soggy digestive biscuit corner in each. In the bedside drawer, there should be a tangle of jewellery, single earrings, dried-up mascara wands, missing batteries (see also 'The Remote Control'), as well as empty blister packs of painkillers. Although sometimes exactly what is inside will remain shrouded in mystery, as the drawer will not open at all.

The clothes in the wardrobe are all old and none of them fit, but cannot be discarded because this is not the Shabby way.

The Wardrobe

The bedroom is a place for the Shabbist to display all recently worn items of clothing. It is essential for these to remain in full view – either on the floor, on a chair, or draped either on – or across the end of – the bed. The clothes in the wardrobe are all old and none of them fit, but cannot be discarded because this is not the Shabby way.

The Underwear Drawer

In Shabbism, the aim of a lady's underwear drawer is to maintain a centrifugal tangle of bras and knickers from which very little can ever successfully or swiftly be removed. Detachable bra straps come in useful to add extra detangling difficulty to the bundle. In the centre of the fray, one often finds a silly fashion bra which has never fitted. A couple of pairs of laddered natural tights frequently finesse the tangle. This drawer often also houses items that are decades old, but can't be thrown away for sentimental or nostalgic reasons (see also 'Shabby Treasures'), such as 'lucky' knickers, and ones that still have your name sewn into them from school.

The Sock Drawer

The aim of the Shabby sock drawer is for it to be perpetually stuffed to the brim with un-matching single socks (see also 'The Sofa'). In this way, the seasoned Shabbist has the daily task of drawer-diving for a wearable pair, amongst the holey-toed, Christmas and novelty socks. Most Shabbists tend to wear odd socks, or no socks, or even just the one sock, as a direct result.

All skilled Shabbists enjoy the challenge and thrill of transforming a humble bedroom into a scene resembling a plane crash.

THE SHABBY BATHROOM

The Shabby bathroom is the showcase for bodged works, messiness and dilapidation, and will always contain at least one 'plughole spider' (see also 'Shabby Pets') that you can't quite face washing away. The porcelain of the sink must be properly stained with limescale residue from a leaky tap, and be adorned with hardened blobs of toothpaste. Toothbrushes must reside either face down on the side of the sink, or in a mug or glass which ideally has at least an inch of unidentifiable brown sludge in the bottom. Plumbing is dodgy throughout, with leaks often ineffectually bandaged with J-cloths.

The Bathroom Cabinet

Shabbists know that cough medicine, like chutney, never goes off, and a full collection of the various types should be stored in the overcrowded bathroom cabinet, along with empty tubs of Vicks and nail varnishes that will never open.

The Shabby bathroom is the showcase for bodged works, messiness and dilapidation.

Because they hate wasting water, being true environmentalists at heart (see also 'Shabby Outdoors' and 'Shabby Fashion'), Shabbists view washing as a necessity and not a hobby and wouldn't dream of spending more than sixty seconds in a shower. Due to poor insulation (generally because of ill-fitting windows), Shabby bathrooms can get very cold and aren't the sort of places you want to hang around in for long.

A GENERAL NOTE ON SHABBY HYGIENE (see also 'Cleanism' and 'The Kitchen Sink')

As a rule, Shabbists don't smell – other than of the garden and cooking – but they don't like to over-wash either. They don't worry at all if they have oil- or paint-stained hands, or soil under their fingernails, and only really need to 'do' their hair or 'have a proper shave' if it's a special occasion. They believe a robust interaction with one's environment results in a resilient immune system. They're not fans of vanity either. Not really giving a damn what other people think, true Shabbists don't look in the mirror very often – and never take selfies – and are said to be much happier and confident for their lack of self-scrutiny.

THE SHABBY LOFT

The loft is a Shabbist's pride and joy – or at least it would be, if they ever had time to visit – and it takes years and years of careful, and indeed not-so-careful cultivation to perfect. Ideally the loft hatch opens far enough for the annual retrieval of the boxes of Christmas and Hallowe'en decorations, but beyond the immediate grab-able area where these are stored, the loft should be a Shabby treasure trove of un-emptied boxes from previous moves, deteriorating rolls of carpet lining, children's prams, cots, toys and grandparents' school reports, as well as every computer and printer ever owned.

It is also home to all the items that are yet to be recycled in the next car-boot sale (see also 'Shabby Entertainment & Hobbies'), but probably never will be.

Central to the landing, and indeed to any Shabbist's heart, is the airing cupboard. A true Shabbist can work on an airing cupboard for a lifetime, carefully concealing such items and keepsakes as crocheted baby blankets, royal wedding tea towels, and possibly explosive, and almost certainly highly toxic, demi-johns of long-forgotten homemade cider and ale. The correct etiquette for the airing cupboard is to achieve a 45-degree (or steeper) angle for the assorted pile of stacked towels and sheets, thereby ensuring that they all fall out every time the door is opened. This is what allows the airing cupboard's contents to be 'aired', thereby giving it its name. The primary rule of the Shabby airing cupboard is that it is impossible to find bedsheets unless every shelf is emptied. Best or guest towels don't belong in the airing cupboard. These should reside over the banisters or on the bedroom chair for swift deployment in the event of a visit.

The Understairs Cupboard

This, along with The Shed, for those Shabbists lucky enough to have a garden, is where the Shabbist's collection of home DIY items are stored, including a full range of nearly empty pots of paint and evaporated white spirit, and jam jars full of solid, paint-clogged brushes, as well as deflated lilos, tennis and badminton rackets (see also 'Shabby Sports'), lidless coolboxes and rusted screwdrivers and saws.

All household cleaning items are also stored here, such as vacuum cleaners and mops, but rather than being allotted a space whereby they could be easily found and removed, these easy-to-access spaces must instead be occupied by rarely used camping equipment,

Vacuum cleaners, mops, buckets and so on should either be precariously balanced, or entirely hidden from view.

with the vacuum cleaners, mops, buckets and so on either precariously balanced on top, or entirely hidden from view.

At floor level, there must be a lethal spill of screws and nails, often cemented to the floor with a leaking grouting gun. Any exposed pipes in the wall area must be stuffed with plastic shopping bags, never-used bags-for-life, and cardboard wine-carriers, along with recycled bubble wrap and Jiffy bags. Truly a Shabby joy to behold.

SHABBY OUTDOORS

As noted earlier, Shabbists are keen environmentalists, insofar as they believe in putting the environment first, because, well, it pretty much sorts itself out, doesn't it? Particularly if people aren't interfering too much with it. After all, it had been there for ages doing perfectly well, thank you very much, before people turned up and started taking advantage of it. Ideally what Shabbists seek is a 'sense of oneness', where environment and person blend happily into one, with neither being overly compromised by the other. Shabbists are also friends of microbes (see 'Note On Shabby Hygiene') and believe that being at one with your Shabby environment boosts both your immune system and general sense of wellbeing and belonging. The great outdoors is, therefore, seen by many Shabbists as a truly Shabby haven, which must be both cherished and adored.

THE SHABBY GARDEN

Skilled Shabbists often like to extend their Shabby skills to the front and back garden, in the event that they have them. A yard can also be given the full Shabby treatment with the addition of some unusable bicycle parts and lethal deckchairs, while balconies and roof terraces can be charmingly and swiftly Shabbified with a few carelessly placed cracked plant pots full of unidentifiable flowers.

Flora & Fauna

The rule of the Shabby garden is that anything that grows, including weeds, should be celebrated, as the Shabbist never actively 'gardens', but rather 'curates', following the well-known Shabby mantra, 'The Garden Gardens Itself.'

That is not to say that a Shabby garden can't be beautiful. Left to its own devices, many Shabby gardens will adopt gorgeous British flora and fauna alike. Walls will be covered in thick ivy, whilst a discarded supermarket rose or pot of rosemary left outside can, in time, form a stunning rambling archway or bush.

The rule of the Shabby garden is that anything that grows, including weeds, should be celebrated, as the Shabbist never actively 'gardens', but rather 'curates'.

Unfinished Projects

The garden is also a good place to look for evidence of the Shabbist's greatest pastime: unfinished projects. These could include evidence of a spring bank holiday flurry of new decking resolve, with the planks still stacked against a wall. Or unopened sacks of tomato- and vegetable-seeded compost from a long-forgotten life decision 'to go fully self-sufficient' this year. All Shabby gardens have at least one abandoned breezeblock and a bag of hard cement, though no one can remember why. All garden furniture should be poorly mended, and/or covered in cobwebs (if housed in The Shed), or splattered with bird excrement (if kept outdoors). Often the Shabby garden sports a saggy washing line, or tilted whirligig, and at least one dangling, homemade bird box that no bird has ever graced with its presence, due to natural self-preservation instincts.

The Lawn

Lawns – as in unified 'shiny', stripy green grass lawns – are anathema to Shabbists, and quietly referred to as 'Wimbledons'. A Shabby lawn should rather be graced with a plethora of plant forms other than grass, such as dandelions, daisies and what-you-will. Lawns will also invariably be patchy and often dug up (see also 'Shabby Pets').

The BBQ

Essential to any Shabby garden is the BBQ (with at least one wheel missing), which remains in the corner of the garden year-round and is home to a wide variety of (possibly poisonous) spiders and bugs. A committed Shabbist will delight in lifting up the lid for the first outdoor feast of the summer to find an atrophied sausage still there on the grill from last year.

The Shabby garden is also home to a wide variety of abandoned children's games and toys, and will usually contain several torn, punctured and gnawed (see also 'Shabby Pets') balls of various shapes and sizes, as well as at least one permanent ring in the grass where a discarded hula-hoop has been depriving it of sunlight, and a far larger circle where the paddling pool was left out over the winter. A jumble of decayed shuttlecocks, missing socks (see also 'The Sock Drawer') and punctured hosepipes will likely complete the Shabby effect, while there's also plenty of potential for Shabby booby-traps (see also 'The Shabby Kitchen'), involving deckchairs and trampolines that have essential parts missing.

Advanced Shabbification (see also 'Note For First-Time Visitors') will also likely be in evidence, with Mother Nature herself advancing deeper each year into the spaces once occupied by man, due to the bluntness of any and all lawnmower blades, loppers, shears, chainsaws and secateurs that the garden's owners may possess. As a result, a Shabby garden is often a riot of colour and birdsong and the buzzing of bees. A truly perfect spot for a cup of Earl Grey tea and a snooze.

THE SHABBY SHED

Novice Shabbists sometimes take refuge in The Shed as a means of hiding from the outside world, with all its responsibilities and woes. But a proper Shabby Shed will be un-inhabitable and often un-enterable, due to its leaky roof and fullness. It's also possible that rodents and foxes will have staked a prior claim to it. At the very least, there should be sizeable colonies of woodlice, spiders and slugs.

The Shed houses many gardening tools that don't work, such as lawnmowers and handle-less spades, as well as leaking tins of creosote, weed-killer and other toxic substances. Plastic sacks full of unidentifiable matter, both liquid and solid, also abound, such as last year's lawn clippings, which have now started self-composting, and rubbish that's still waiting for someone to take it to the dump.

SHABBY ON THE MOVE

Much like home, the car should be a temple to Shabbism and provides ample scope and opportunity for disciples of the faith to display its Four Central Pillars in all their manifest glory. At the very least, the Shabbist should ensure their vehicle contains enough discarded food and detritus to allow them to survive a crash into a snowdrift until they thaw out in spring. The boot should always be full of flaking, dried, mud-crusted single wellies as well as pine needles from Christmas trees past that were shed during their journey to the dump. The Shabbist driver's ultimate goal? Their very own car mice, which can survive right there alongside them in that snowdrift too.

A perfect addition to any garden, hallway or yard is a collection of un-usable, un-roadworthy bikes. These should be 'rediscovered' each spring with much excitement, only to be returned to their tangle once it's remembered that they don't actually work.

Camping (aka 'Shamping')

In many ways, the aesthetic opposite of glamping. The Shabby attitude to camping is old school. The Shabbist eschews comfort in favour of a tussle with the elements, due to the innate paucity of all Shabby equipment and packing errors. Pure Shabbists will have an assortment of jumbled camping equipment to hand at all time (see also 'The Understairs Cupboard') and relish every opportunity to embrace the great outdoors, even if the weather forecast is iffy.

The Shabby camper will never have enough tent pegs to actually erect their tent, relying on a handful of defunct pegs, along with welcome donations from less-Shabby friends, to pin the main points. Tents should always leak in the rain. Most Shabbists are perfectly prepared for their tent to fully wash away at some point.

SHABBY SPORTS

Shabbists tend to take a haphazard approach at best to formal exercise. Why use a step counter when your legs will let you know in their own good time when they've had enough? It is the Shabby way to be full of good intentions, but a lack of competitiveness and the right equipment and time often means these intentions are never met, and the only actual regular form of exercise taken is the walk to the pub (see also 'Shambling').

As affected by New Year's Day hangover guilt as the next person, Shabbists occasionally sign up for gym membership in January in a flurry of enthusiasm, but go only the once. (However, they do then keep the direct debit going forever on the off-chance that the exercise muse might descend.)

The Shabby way is also to spot a bargain, so secondhand exercise bikes, rowing

machines, or weird sit-up contraptions may be purchased on a whim at car-boot sales. These will break almost immediately and will be mothballed, along with any other sporting equipment purchased over the years (see also 'The Utility Room').

This is not, however, to say that Shabbists can't be sporty. Far from it. In the summer, Shabbists often embrace their inner tennis champion and come out with their ancient school rackets for a knock-up in the park. Or meet friends for a picnic and a spot of touch rugby with a slightly deflated ball, or a game of French cricket with a dog-chewed bat.

The correct Shabby attire for these sporting occasions is as follows:
Men: Old paint-splattered trainers with no grip. Rock band T-shirt (must be at least twenty years old). Tracksuit bottoms or shorts (which have doubled many times as pyjama bottoms).

Women: Baggy sports bra (or possibly two old bras worn at once in an attempt to increase much-needed support). Sports top that's been sprayed with perfume due to permanent underarm whiff, despite the many washes. Unflattering leggings with holes. Borrowed trainers, possibly belonging to a child.

Shambling (aka A Jolly Good Walk)

The Shabbist firmly believes that a giant Sunday roast accompanied by a few daytime pints or glasses of wine are completely negated (in terms of healthiness) by a constitutional yomp. These walks, while spontaneous, are also compulsory and involve all family members and friends, usually with the secret aim of heading to a faraway pub.

The rules of these 'Shambling' expeditions are as follows:

1. There should be no map, because 'it's obvious, right', where you're all heading.
2. Mobile phones with anything more than 2 per cent battery are not allowed.
3. All pre-filled bottles of tap water should always be accidentally left in the boot next to the broken kite.
4. Small children should have inappropriate footwear, but an excess of outer layers that the adults have to lug for the duration of the Shamble.
5. Any ball that is taken for the dog should get lost within the first five minutes.
6. Nobody should be prepared for the rain, yet it will always rain.
7. The walk in question should be at least three miles longer than anyone was expecting.

SHABBY LIFESTYLE

'Be part of life, not
apart from it.'
Ancient Shabbist Proverb

SHABBY PARENTING

For the greater glory of Shabbism, the ultimate goal of Shabby parents
is to produce Shabby kids – the kind of children who throw their
anoraks at the coat pegs and miss (see also 'The Shabby Welcome'), or
merrily tread mud through the hallway, and are capable of entertaining
themselves for several hours in the Shabby Garden playing Swingball
with two rackets without any string. These happy, Shabby children are
the very same ones destined to smear silly putty all over the furniture and
discard their school uniforms in the hallway upon entering the home.
They're also known to dance to scratched records and read books in the
warm patch (see also 'The Shabby Kitchen'). In every sense, they truly are
the Shabby apples of their Shabby parents' eyes.

The ultimate goal of Shabby parents is to produce Shabby kids – the kind of children who throw their anoraks at coat pegs – and miss.

The trick to Shabby parenting is to make it look as if you've made an effort with your kids, when in fact you haven't, and they are, rather, completely feral. But there are many other ways to spot a Shabby parent too …

Shabby parents never travel with the requisite amount of nappies and baby paraphernalia. That's what friends are for.

The proper Shabby look for a buggy is upturned; its toddler will recently have vacated its seat without any prior warning, causing all the blue plastic bags full of booze from the offie that were hanging from the handles to upend the entire vehicle.

By the time the little darlings get to school, Shabby practices should come naturally. Such as writing their names directly on their supermarket-bought, non-regulation uniform in biro, rather than ever ordering name-tags.

The Shabby way is to celebrate the free stuff. There is never any need to buy a formal school photograph, when the sample they send is perfectly fridge-door worthy.

All children of Shabbists will have nits at some stage in their lives – or quite possibly throughout their entire lives, depending on the child. The aim of the Shabbist is to make sure that the child is combed out once, but to always leave that second (crucial) combing until a few days later (due to lack of time and patience), thereby ensuring that the nits are given ample opportunity to proliferate. Shabbists never admit to their children having nits and the children themselves are taught early on to blame other children for their affliction.

SHABBY FASHION

It has been frequently noted that many Shabbists regard themselves and their environments as indivisible. The one blends into the other (see 'sense of oneness' in 'Shabby Outdoors'), so much so that it's entirely possible to visit a Shabbist's home and not even notice them sitting on their stained, torn sofa in their frayed, patched jacket.

Proper Shabbists believe in wearing their clothes to death – and indeed at their own funerals too. All Shabbists firmly believe that quality items (particularly outer garments) never go out of fashion. This is an extreme form of recycling, known as 'me-cycling', where Shabbists keep once fashionable clothing at the bottom of wardrobes (often for decades) until they're back in, or bequeath un-thrown-out clothing to their children or indeed to friends as re-gifts. Men should be proud to wear jackets with frayed cuffs, whilst Shabbist women often rock the same leather jacket for a lifetime. All coats and jacket pockets should contain loose change, old tissues, one mint or sweet – the last in the packet – and several poo bags (for dogs; see 'Shabby Pets').

The Shabby look is not only very comfortable, but transcends class. Sometimes the poshest, richest people are also the most Shabby. In a nutshell, being Shabby means achieving a look that is the opposite of Shiny or groomed. Clothes should be 'lived-in', like one's face.

The Shabby way is to embrace vintage. Being far too busy to shop for clothes as a pastime, a true Shabbist likes to buy good-quality clothes, but only rarely, and will keep them forever. He or she will happily wear a faithful little black dress or donkey jacket to scores of events over the years, dressing it up or down to make it look a little different each time. The reason old style never goes out of fashion is because it's clothing you've had a good time in before, which delivers its own air of confidence. The response to any compliment should always be a modest, 'What this old thing? I've had it for years.' Modesty, economy, and anti-Shininess at its very best.

SHABBY EATING

Shabbists are great entertainers and love to cook for family and friends (see also 'Shabby Entertainment & Hobbies'). Nothing ever goes to waste – even the smallest amount of leftovers is decanted into cereal bowls and cling-filmed in the fridge.

Left to their own devices, Shabbists enjoy the following as some of the mainstays of their diet:

The 'Leftovers' Supper
These are the most creative of suppers and can often be made into something really special with the addition of a fried or poached egg, as well as fridge condiments such as piccalilli or spiced rhubarb chutney. King amongst the leftover suppers is, of course, bubble and squeak, using Sunday's roast potatoes and all the veg.

The 'On Toast' Supper
This means something, usually tinned, 'on toast'. Although the toast part will be the remaining crusty ends of a stale loaf of bread.

Favourite toppings include: packet noodles, bog-standard cheddar, baked beans, sardines or pilchards in tomato sauce, or extremely ripe Stilton – enjoyed singularly or, ideally, together.

The Fridge Lunch

Delve deep enough and a Shabbist can often rustle up a feast of delights from the fridge at any given time. The trick is to 'mix and match' and not worry too much about whether different foods should go together, just whether they do. A classic Shabby fridge lunch might include, for example, some microwaved biryani from last night's curry served up with cauliflower cheese and a wedge of pork pie left over from last Saturday's picnic to use as an improvised scoop – all, of course, with a squirt of mayonnaise and Tabasco on top.

Pasta Surprise

This is a great family supper and involves finishing up all the packets of pasta in the cupboard at once. Spaghetti, penne, fusilli, tagliatelle, in green, white, orange, black or brown – all are welcome here. To be accompanied by the scrapings from several of the almost-certainly-already-opened-but-not-actually-finished jars of pesto in the fridge, along with a 'multi-grating' of the several equally-almost-certainly-opened-but-not-yet-finished bars of Parmesan and Grana Padano. Served with a gherkin on top.

SHABBY ENTERTAINMENT & HOBBIES

The Shabby way is often homemade, and there's no exception in entertainment. Shabbists can be quite impulsive – due to their frequent messiness of thought, known as 'mindlessness' – and are perfectly capable of taking up new hobbies at a moment's notice. For example, after some bargain hunting at a car-boot sale, there may be a flurry of enthusiasm for, say, canoeing or kite-surfing, or kit-car making. Or darts. The lack of space available at home to do these hobbies is not a hindrance to the Shabbist's enthusiasm.

Underlying all Shabbist entertainment and hobbies is their love of socialising – it being the opposite of work – and here are some of the top ways they do it.

Shabby Entertaining

Shabbists love entertaining at home. For them it's an entirely un-stressful experience, because they don't really care if other people make a mess, so long as they have a good time. Shabbists also tend to un-cultivate friends who give a damn if there are crumbs on the kitchen table. Not worrying about how things look frees up the Shabbist to drill down to what actually matters, namely how people feel and what's going on. For the very reason that it is so easy to put your feet up and relax in a Shabbist's home, you'll often find that they have lots of friends. Shabbist get-togethers tend to involve everyone mucking in, lots of drinking, food, laughter and music. A Shabby party is usually a very happy one.

The Pub

Pubs are what make Britain great, and many of them are properly and wonderfully Shabby. The best are the ones with no televisions or Wi-Fi, with scuffed-up furniture and worn carpets, a friendly dog and/or cat, lots of trinkets and artwork on display and some welcoming staff who love a chat whilst they are pouring a tipple of sherry or a pint of ale.

The pub garden should always be Shabby too, with worn benches and patchy grass. Truly a home from home, it should reflect the Shabbist's home environment as much as possible.

Car-Boot Sales

The heady combination of finding a bargain and something wonderful to put on show in the home is why Shabbists embrace the car-boot sale with such enthusiasm. Shabbists are naturally curious (indeed envious) regarding other people's clutter, and if they're competitive in any way at all, it's in measuring up their own 'Shabby Treasures' (see also 'The Shabby Kitchen') against those of their peers. If finding themselves in the highly unusual position of selling items (see also 'The Shabby Loft'), most Shabbists will find it hard to actually part with anything at all, regardless of the amount of money they are offered. In this regard, it's been suggested that Shabbists only actually go to car-boot sales at all to show off their Shabby treasures and accumulate others. Most Shabbists will admit to always taking home more from a car-boot sale than they brought with them to sell.

Fêtes & Fairs

Combining elements of the pub and the car-boot sale, the village or park fête is a truly British affair and a delight to many Shabbists, who can show off their homemade wares and eccentricity with pride, along with sampling the beverages and vittles of their contemporaries. The general air of chaos and amateurism on show also feeds directly into their love, indeed worship, of messiness, dilapidation, clutter and bodged works (see also 'The Four Central Pillars').

Playing Games

Shabbists love a board game – in fact, anything that doesn't need batteries, which of course can never be found (see also 'The Remote Control') – and actively encourage playing games with their family and friends. Quite often, however, there will be crucial pieces of these games missing (see also 'The Living Room Rug'), so Shabbists make up their own games. The name game, or identifying the first line of a song and singing the second line, are particular favourites. Along with sardines, clothes-line badminton, and 'What's in the Jar?' (see also 'The Fridge').

Reading

Shabbists love books and particularly like to collect books about hobbies they may yet take up, but probably never will – such as needlepoint, tapestry, mountain hiking and langlaufing. There should always be a pile of eclectic books (often humorous) in the downstairs loo in a Shabby home, known affectionately as 'The Lav Library', and always on hand in an emergency should the real lavatory paper run out.

Music

Most Shabbists would admit to preferring the era of rotary phones and Sony Walkmans, and it is rare to find a surround-sound system that actually works. There may be attempts to instal technology as the years go by, but they invariably fail, whereupon Shabbists happily resort to old-school methods, such as the radio or record player. Or indeed by making music themselves. There is often an out-of-tune piano, guitar or ukulele in the vicinity for this purpose. And sometimes a kazoo.

Home-Brewing & Jam-Making

All Shabbists have a go at these, as they hate the idea of waste, and any sudden crop of wild blackberries, elderflowers or apples that appears in a Shabby garden, or a nearby field, must be made into something – then smeared on toast, or drunk.

SHABBY AT WORK

The Shabby Commute
This should begin with a daily morning panic looking for the rail pass, phone, a pair of un-laddered tights and pants, resulting in breakfast being eaten on the hoof, poor concentration and missed stops.

The Shabby Desk
The Shabbist's desk at work should be piled high with papers and books and important Post-it notes stuck on the screen of the computer, the keyboard of which is grubby and fully of crumbs. Underneath the desk, female Shabbists will house a large pile of shoes, which are so painful to wear, they are only deployed to totter from the desk to the meeting room and/or pub and back. It is not uncommon for a Shabbist to hastily don mismatching shoes on these occasions.

The desk drawer, if openable, is part of the general Shabby filing system, which includes emails; the guiding principle is that the lower down something is, the less likely it is to be dealt with. Or, to put it another way, Shabbists abhor the modern work practice of GIGO (Garbage In, Garbage Out), preferring to operate on the principle of GI-LOW.

The Shabby Meeting
Total lack of preparation for any important meeting often results in the intense quizzing of others. While being, in fact, a deflection technique, this is often mistaken as brilliant management, resulting in the accidental over-promotion of the Shabbist, to the bemusement of the Shinies.

It's also common to see a Shabby employee attempting to change the subject of a meeting, or indeed to undermine the very purpose of a meeting, in order to gain equal footing with other employees who've actually done their homework.

Combined with the Shabbist's natural aversion to rules and regulation, and their contrasting attraction to chaos and creativity, such behaviour during meetings can result in Shabbists inadvertently attaining guru-like reputations as corporate and industrial disruptors (see also 'accidental over-promotion' above).

The Shabby Work Lunch

Lunch should begin in the pub at one minute past noon and conclude no sooner than four. At no point during the Shabby work lunch should work itself be discussed.

Shabby Self-Employment

Many Shabbists naturally reject the notion of working for 'the man' and instead embark on (often financially disastrous) self-employment ruses. As well as giving themselves ample scope for messiness, clutter and bodged works, this means they get to wear what they want (which generally means whatever it was they were wearing the day before).

But even when working from home, the occasional need to scrub up arises. Such as on a video call to a person with a proper job. On these occasions, the Shabbist will often 'go half-and-half', meaning they'll wear a suit jacket, shirt and tie where the camera can see their top half, but not their tea-stained joggers or boxers below.

Shabbists love their pets, and animal ownership chimes with the Shabby way of life (see also 'The Four Central Pillars' of messiness, dilapidation, clutter and bodged works). Quite often a Shabbist's home will be filled with dogs, cats, guinea pigs and goldfish (but not necessarily all in the same room).

Dogs in a Shabby home are rarely washed, but left to self-clean in their bed or by rubbing against the sofa cushions (see also 'The Living Room'). They tend to keep their teeth clean by gnawing at the furniture (see also 'The Kitchen Table').

Cats are given free access to all areas in the Shabby home and can sharpen their claws on any home furnishings, particularly those in a prominent position (see also 'The Living Room').

Fish make marvellous pets and suit the Shabbist way entirely. They are low-maintenance and require very little effort from their owners.

Seasoned Shabbists will open cage doors and let pets – even small ones, such as guinea pigs – roam freely around the home. Warning: guinea pigs may grow in size with this practice due to their partialness to dog kibble.

A SHABBY CHRISTMAS

Shabbists love Christmas as it's a chance to partake in many of their favourite hobbies all at once (see also 'Shabby Entertainment & Hobbies'). Hosting less Shabbily minded members of the extended family can lead to some pre-Christmas stress, but at these times a Shabbist should be reminded of the Four Central Pillars and not give a flying damn about what a judgemental aunty, sister or mother-in-law thinks, and simply crack open the homemade sloe gin instead.

A SHABBY FAREWELL

With wave upon wave of new lifestyle fads currently attempting to undermine our home-grown British ways, it's important to remember that there's something reassuringly trustworthy and innately comforting about being Shabby. It's a way of life that's both tried and tested, reliable and forgiving – much like a favourite saucepan, an old mate or even a faithful hound.

So next time you consider beating yourself up about your home not being tidier or shinier, stop and breathe. Embrace your inner Shabbist. Celebrate what actually is, rather than what could be if you only spent a little bit more of your time and effort cleaning and sorting.

After all, time makes everything – and everyone – Shabby eventually, so why not try to just go with the flow? Get the wine out of the fridge – if you can find it – or put the kettle on. Put your feet up on the kitchen table, alongside all that other stuff, and look around. Relax. Everything you see in your messy, loving, gloriously cluttered abode makes it your home. And that's just fine because …

Shabby = Happy